IMAGES
of America

PEORIA

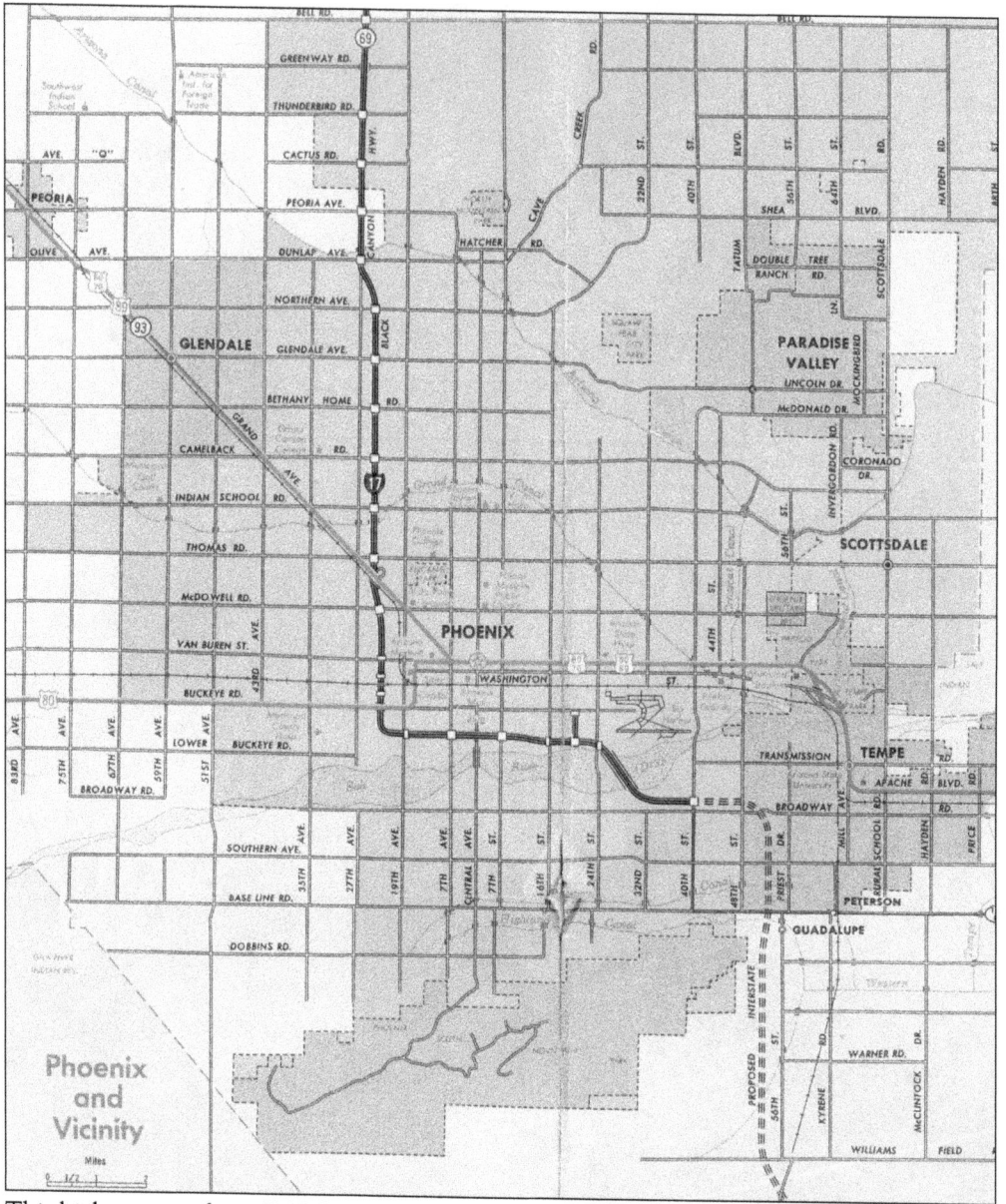

This highway map from 1966 shows Peoria in relation to Glendale and Phoenix, Arizona, along U.S. Highway 60 (Grand Avenue). In 1960, Peoria's population hovered at 2,600. By 1970, the city had only gained about 2,000 residents. Growth came from two directions: Sun City, the nation's first retirement community which opened north of Peoria in 1960, and Glendale and Phoenix, which began expanding their borders by annexing land. Peoria's farmland was slowly converted to neighborhoods, and by 2000, the city had a population of 108,000. (Courtesy of Arizona Highway Department.)

ON THE COVER: The Peoria General Store was located at the southeast corner of Washington Street and Eighty-third Avenue. This photograph was most likely taken before the fire of 1917 that inspired the town to build with brick. R. A. Tuckey, who moved with his wife, Addie, from Minnesota around 1892, operated the store. (Courtesy of Peoria Arizona Historical Society.)

IMAGES
of America

PEORIA

Jodey Elsner and the
Peoria Arizona Historical Society

ARCADIA
PUBLISHING

Published by Arcadia Publishing
Charleston, South Carolina

Library of Congress Control Number: 2009921910

For all general information contact Arcadia Publishing at:
Telephone 843-853-2070
Fax 843-853-0044
E-mail sales@arcadiapublishing.com
For customer service and orders:
Toll-Free 1-888-313-2665

Visit us on the Internet at www.arcadiapublishing.com

This book is dedicated to the pioneers of Peoria who cultivated the desert and grew a community. It is also dedicated to my parents, Steve and Claire, who encouraged me to develop my love of history into a career.

CONTENTS

ACKNOWLEDGMENTS

In small towns all over Arizona, historical societies provide an invaluable service. Volunteers collect and categorize the documents and artifacts of the past and operate museums, ably chronicling the history of their towns. This is often undertaken with minimal or no outside assistance, either by professionals or funding. These special organizations are not lauded and appreciated enough for all that they do.

The Peoria Arizona Historical Society is one of these organizations. The one-time farming community grew to become a large suburb of the fifth largest city in the country. Yet the society trudges along with the same limited budget and same volunteers, doing their best to preserve Peoria's past and sharing it with an ever-growing and evolving population.

All of the photographs in this book are from the collection of the Peoria Arizona Historical Society and were originally collected and categorized by its volunteers. Numerous Peoria families donated these photographs. The collection of the historical society is only as thorough as those who have decided to donate to it. There are families with little documentation in the collection, and this is a shame. Perhaps someone reading this with ties to Peoria's past will recall the family photographs in the closet and come forward with yet another piece of the town's history.

Of the selfless volunteers who support the Peoria Arizona Historical Society and this project, none has been more helpful than Harold McKisson, a Peoria native. Harold, along with his wife, Vicki, both cheerfully answered off-the-cuff questions on Peoria and its people during the research process. They provided their assistance tirelessly, just as they do for the historical society.

Many thanks also go out to Jared Jackson at Arcadia Publishing for his thoughtful editing and support throughout the process.

INTRODUCTION

The Hohokam people were spread across the Salt River Valley in settlements near seasonal waterways that flowed with consistency before the dams of the 20th century were built. The remains of some of the largest permanent settlements were discovered in downtown Phoenix in conjunction with large-scale construction projects. In Peoria, sites dating as far back as 1,000 years ago have been discovered, lending more information to the valley's ancient history. The Hohokam disappeared from the valley sometime around 1450.

Like the ancient people who came before, Peoria's success has hinged on the availability of water. With water, the desert yields abundant crops. It is no wonder early white settlers irrigated the desert via canals and created a rich agricultural region, just as the Hohokam did. Former Confederate soldier Jack Swilling was inspired by the remnants of the Hohokam canal system and built his own in Phoenix in the 1860s. As the small town grew, other towns around it began to develop around the Salt River Valley for much the same reason.

William J. Murphy, as lead contractor and fund-raiser for the Arizona Canal Company, was instrumental in bringing water to the area northwest of Phoenix. The 41-mile-long Arizona Canal, completed in 1885, made it possible for homesteaders to irrigate their land and grow crops. The canal, still in use today, extends from the Salt River northeast of Mesa at the Granite Reef Dam to Peoria near the intersection of Seventy-fifth Avenue and Greenway Road. In 1887, Murphy and a handful of backers founded the Arizona Improvement Company, a development company created to encourage settlers to locate to land served by the Arizona Canal. The Arizona Improvement Company also constructed Grand Avenue. Completed in the summer of 1888, the road was described by the *Phoenix Daily Herald* as "straight as a line, level as a floor." The same men who built the waterways for the Arizona Canal Company laid the roadbed.

Murphy marketed the area to residents of Peoria, Illinois, among other cities in the country, networking with acquaintances to gain entrée to possible investors. He touted the canal and the possibility of rich agriculture, as well as the veritable blank slate the area offered. Some 5,000 acres in northwestern Salt River Valley was sold to residents of Peoria, Illinois, and in the fall of 1886, Peorians from Illinois left for the west to establish what would become Peoria, Arizona.

Grand Avenue was built to accommodate a future railroad line between Phoenix and Prescott, which passed through Peoria in the early 1890s. At that time, Peoria was a collection of impermanent buildings. The town was not officially platted until 1897. This allowed settlers to purchase a tenth of an acre lot to build their own home. Prior to the standardized avenue and street numbering of the 1960s, Peoria had picturesque names for its north-south streets: Walnut Street (Eighty-first Avenue), Vine Street (Eighty-second Avenue), Orange Street (Eighty-third Avenue), Olive Street, (Eighty-third Drive), Peach Street (Eighty-fourth Avenue), and Almond Street (Eighty-fifth Avenue).

Through the beginning of the 20th century, Peoria's downtown slowly began to resemble a permanent settlement. The town well received a water tower for storage in 1894. The commercial area fronting Grand Avenue offered retail shopping for the town's early residents, supplies for local farmers, and provisions for travelers up and down Grand Avenue. The train depot served passengers and freight. If it could not be found in Peoria, Glendale, or Phoenix, it could be shipped via the Santa Fe, Prescott, and Phoenix Railroad.

Most of Peoria's residents lived outside the original plat. They were farmers and ranchers scattered throughout the desert, which was then being aggressively cultivated. After the construction of the Roosevelt Dam in 1911, the likelihood of seasonal flooding was greatly diminished. The northwest portion of the Salt River Valley began to look like the rest of the Phoenix basin, verdant and idyllic.

In the summer of 1917, a fire destroyed the majority of Peoria's commercial district. Most buildings were of pressed metal and wood. After the fire, however, the overwhelming building material of choice became brick. Many of these brick buildings, like those lining Washington Street, still stand (although they have undergone extensive remodeling).

Cotton was introduced during World War I, becoming the primary crop grown around Peoria. Gins sprouted up to process the crop, and a mini-construction boom took place in the new prosperity. Although the bottom fell out of the cotton market in 1920, Peorians recovered. The Edwards Hotel was constructed, along with the Women's Club and the Hood Building during this time.

The Great Depression slowed the town's growth. Works Progress Administration (WPA) projects, as part of Pres. Franklin D. Roosevelt's New Deal program, enhanced the small settlement, constructing a jail building in 1937. Peoria's population fluctuated with the arrival and departure of Dust Bowl refugees. World War II brought an influx of soldiers to Luke Air Force Base, located just west of Peoria. A housing shortage promoted backyard apartments and additions to homes to accommodate the new residents.

Peoria prospered in the 1950s. The automobile travelers that utilized Grand Avenue stopped in Peoria for gas, repairs, and food. Peoria was the last major stop before Wickenburg from Phoenix and flourished because of it. At that time and prior to the construction of the interstate highway system, Grand Avenue was the route for State Highway 93 and U.S. Highways 60, 70, and 89.

In 1954, Peoria was incorporated as a town, solidifying the settlement's permanence. Farm fields gave way to neighborhoods, although pockets of agriculture can still be found today. Phoenix and Scottsdale annexed county land at a rapid pace in the 1950s, and soon towns like Glendale and Peoria were also caught up in the expansion frenzy. The construction of Sun City, beginning in 1960, spurred construction in nearby Peoria. In the decade between 1980 and 1990, the population of Peoria had increased 300 percent and was now a full-fledged city. From 1990 to 2007, Peoria nearly tripled in size once more.

In just over 100 years, the modest agricultural settlement has become Arizona's ninth largest city. The city continues to expand in land and population, offering opportunities much as it did a century ago.

One

FAMILIAR FACES

Joseph B. Greenhut (pictured at right) and Deloss S. Brown owned the land that would become the town of Peoria. In 1890, that amounted to four sections of land equalling 2,560 acres. According to the terms of the land acquisition from the federal government, the men were required to make certain improvements in order to gain full title to the land. Greenhut and Brown platted the town in 1897.

Hiram C. Mann was superintendent of the Greenhut Ranch. Mann helped found the first school in Peoria in 1889, which, after statehood in 1912, would become School District 11 in the state of Arizona. Mann would later operate his own ranch at the corner of Olive and Grand Avenues. His bungalow, built around 1910, stood at the southwestern corner of the intersection before Grand Avenue was widened and the home was torn down.

Jennie and Hiram Mann briefly lived in a former store building in downtown Peoria west of the corner of Washington Street and Eighty-third Avenue. When better accommodations were made available for the two on the Greenhut Ranch, they moved there. Their former home briefly became the first location of the First Presbyterian Church of Peoria. Jennie, pictured at right, began the town's Sunday school.

Ethel Marie Prugh posed in 1919 for what was likely her wedding portrait before marrying Walter A. "Doc" Lewis. In the early 1930s, she was a librarian at Peoria High School and was active in the Women's Club and other social organizations. The Lewises lived north of Thunderbird Road on Seventy-fifth Avenue when the road was known as Lateral 20 for the waterway that ran along it.

James Weed is seated with his grandchildren James and Rachel. The pioneering Weed family came from Kansas and founded the Old Paths Bible School near Seventy-fifth Avenue and Thunderbird Road in 1912. The property is now owned by Southwest Indian Ministries. The Weeds, along with the Pomeroys, Postlewaits, Calhouns, Claudsons, Sharps, and the McKissons, among others, also ran a broom-making operation on the site.

These unidentified residents of the area surrounding the Old Paths Bible School known as Weedville pose on a tractor at an unknown date. The property consisted of 160 acres divided among eight families. The Old Paths Bible School also operated a newspaper, all issues of which are housed at the Peoria Arizona Historical Society.

The Old Paths Bible School buildings can be seen behind the trees. The handwritten message on the back of this photograph reads, "Beulah, this is Old Paths. Who is it? Jimmy, Faye, Boyd, and Bobby?" Weedville is roughly 3 miles from downtown Peoria. At the time of this photograph, the trip would have been along dirt roads with only farmland along the way.

Holidays were cause for people to gather and celebrate. Neighbors were spread far and wide during Peoria's early days, and this was often the only time many families would see one another, unless they were regular churchgoers. Members of the Puckett and Crawford families gathered for a Fourth of July picnic in 1913. The wagon was for hauling hay, not people.

Marvin Lewis Varney, age 10, sits astride his horse, possibly at the family's farm. Children learned horsemanship at a very young age and took part in chores around the farm to help sustain their families. The date of this photograph is *c.* 1932.

Before air conditioning became commonplace in homes in the 1950s, people were left to their own devices to cool themselves in the summertime. Ken Johnson, left, and his brother Roy slept outside on cots in the 1940s and hoped for a breeze. Sleeping porches were common on houses and hotels at the time. Ken and Roy made do with the lawn.

School pageants and plays were a form of entertainment for communities removed from larger towns. The Peoria Women's Club mounted a production of *Tom Thumb's Wedding* in the grammar school auditorium on May 12, 1925. The mock wedding was a popular play in the 1920s and had a cast only of children younger than 10 years.

Sybil and O. K. Leonard purchased Peoria's only movie theater in 1947 after it suffered a fire. The theater was originally known as the Paramount, constructed in 1920 and operated by O. O. Fuel. The one-screen theater later became Peoria Fire Station No. 1. It was located between the two-story Hood Building and the Peoria/Edwards Hotel on Washington Street downtown. The building still stands but as of 2010 is vacant.

Orville and Priscilla Cook posed for their wedding portrait in 1937. The Cooks were both active in Peoria's political and organizational history. Orville served as mayor in the 1970s while Priscilla was president of the Women's Club. As of 2010, she volunteers at the historical society and sits on the Peoria Historic Preservation Commission among other activities.

Alfredo "Freddie" Duarte was born near the corner of Eighty-third Avenue and Northern Avenue in 1926. Not long after, his family moved downtown. Freddie played trumpet and began to hone his musical talent as a student at Central School (now the historical society). Freddie assembled his own band in 1953.

The Orquesta de Freddie Duarte (Freddie Duarte's Orchestra) played Latin-based big band music at ballrooms and nightclubs across the country. The popular dance music was featured on Sunday nights at Phoenix's largest dance venue, the Riverside Ballroom, where Freddie also played. Freddie's group disbanded in 1964, but he remained a musician throughout the rest of his life. He died in 1995.

From left to right, Laverne, Francis, and Bill Turner stand next to an Essex auto with Peoria farm fields in the background. The Turner family literally helped build the community through their construction company, particularly downtown.

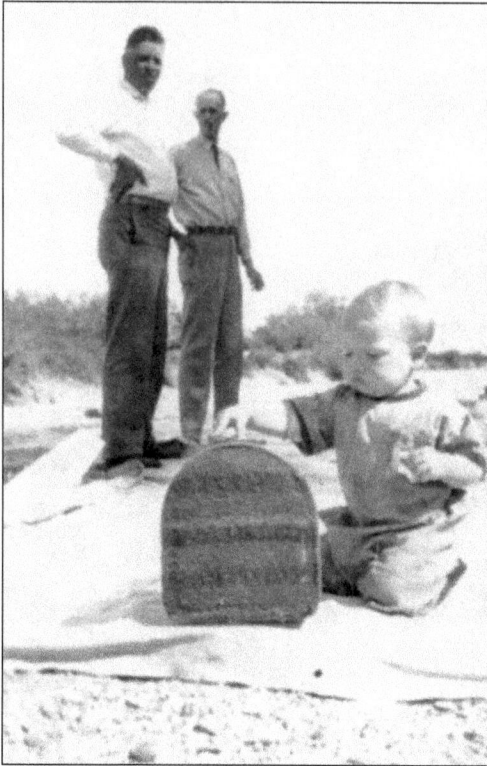

Peoria native Don Bissinger plays with a basket at a family picnic in March 1927. Behind him are Mr. Ellsworth (left) and Don's father, George L. "Bing" Bissinger (right).

Don Bissinger's family photographs include this shot of him behind the bumper of the family car. Don became a farmer, like his father, and married Betty Moore.

Men of the 77th Infantry Division pose for a photograph during World War II. Don Bissinger is at the center of the photograph. Don, a student at Arizona State University prior to the war, fought at the invasion of Okinawa, Japan.

From left to right, Helen Turner, Georgia Deatsch (on flagpole), and Avis Varney Chaney clown around the flagpole in front of the main building at Peoria High School.

From left to right, June Ellen (Reed) Puckett, a girl named Alice, and an unidentified woman paused for a snapshot in 1944. June was a riveter during World War II at the Goodyear Plant and married Harmon Puckett in 1947.

Nala, an unidentified woman, and Alice stopped by June Ellen (Reed) Puckett's house for a visit in 1944.

Albert Wharton made violins in his workshop at 8290 West Madison Street. The former farmer moved from Arkansas to Peoria in 1930. Here he is operating a violin router, part of the violin construction process.

James and Irene Montoya show off their new baby, James Jr., in 1947. The Montoyas are standing in front of their home on Eighty-fourth Avenue, across from present-day city hall. At the time, Eighty-fourth Avenue was named Peach Street.

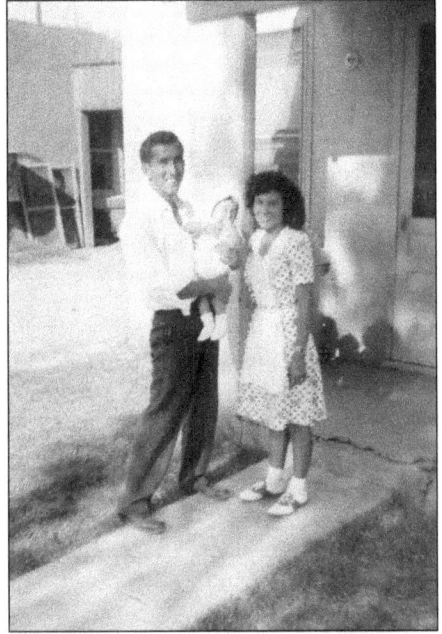

Little Kathy Montoya-Moore sits atop the family's 1949 Chevrolet in 1953. Her father, James "Jimmy" Montoya Sr., operated Jimmy's Signs for 40 years.

From left to right, Lena Grace, Irene, and Bessie Young show off their bicycles purchased from Wood's Pharmacy, run by the Vickery family, in 1945. The location of the photograph is a home on Jefferson Street.

The Women's Club was among the first organizations in Peoria, founded in 1918. Their clubhouse was constructed in 1920 and originally located near the corner of Eighty-third Avenue and Washington Street. The building hosted the town's first library and was a temporary movie house in the early 1920s. Mrs. Elmer Horton, Mrs. Otis Cook, Mrs. V. W. Davidson, Mrs. Charles Stone, Mrs. O. K. Wolfenbarger, Mrs. C. W. Boyle, and Mrs. Elsie Nicoll meet at the clubhouse in 1951. The building was moved to the corner of Eighty-fourth Avenue and Jefferson Street in 2008.

Edmund "Ed" Tang managed the Sun Maid grocery store for his parents from 1953 through 1962. He purchased the store from his parents in 1962. It was located in the one-story commercial row along Washington Street in downtown Peoria. In 1979, Edmund was elected mayor of Peoria and served until 1985.

From left to right, postal workers Wilcie Stone, Bill Daly, and Wayne Bradshaw are seen here in the 1950s when the post office was located in the Brice Building on Grand Avenue near Wilhelm's Garage. The post office would get a brand new home almost two decades later.

Christmas at the post office was surely a stressful and busy time. The employees had a moment to pose for a quick photograph in 1955. From left to right are (first row) Gene Mason and Wayne Bradshaw; (second row) Ed Forney, Gene Reynolds, Bob Turner, Wilbur Thorton, Georgia Scrivner, and Wilcie Stone.

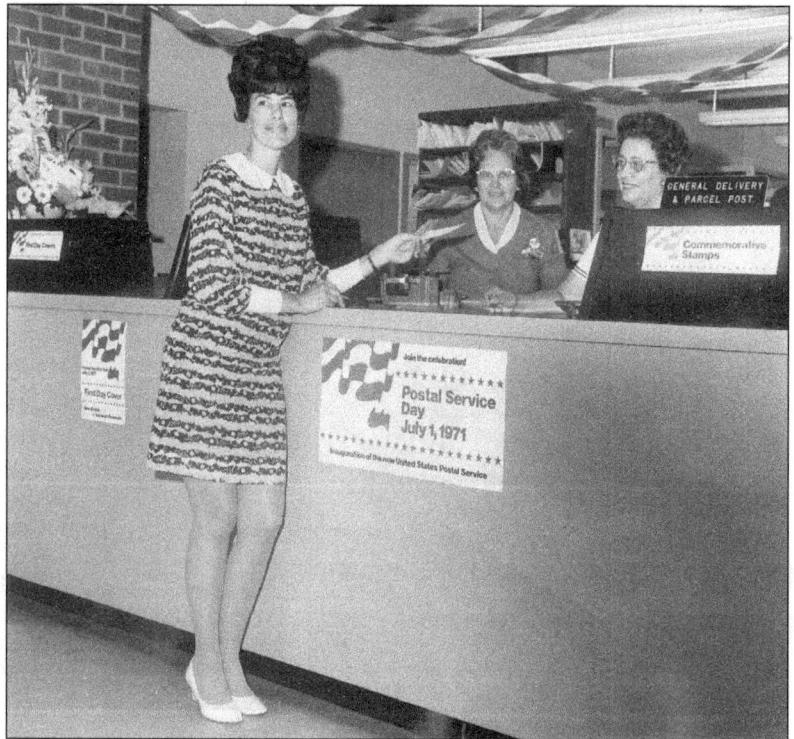

The new post office was cause for celebration for Peorians. In 1971, Mrs. Marshall (left) of the Arizona Bank hands a letter to postmaster Wilcie Stone (center) and clerk Georgia Scrivner (right).

From left to right are Stan Ward, Wayne Bradshaw, and George Davis. Wayne Bradshaw retired from the Peoria Post Office on October 18, 1980, after 33 years of service. Bradshaw was postmaster of Peoria in the 1970s. He also signed up as a volunteer firefighter in 1952 and served as a city councilman from 1983 to 1987.

Folklorico is a form of Hispanic folk dancing. These Peoria youngsters happily pose in their Western costumes, ready to dance at a moment's notice.

Sheryl Bodenstedt (left) chauffered grand marshal Toni Lebario (right) in the September 1987 Mexican Fiesta Parade. Toni was the longtime owner of Toni's Beauty Shoppe on Eighty-third Avenue, just south of the Hood Building downtown.

Former Arizona governor and broadcaster Jack Williams (left) was the grand marshal at Peoria's Centennial Parade on April 12, 1986. Vera May Williams (right) rides along with her husband down Washington Street with the former Peoria Hotel in the background.

Two

BUILDING A TOWN

The Blue Mill Café was the first permanent building in Peoria. It was constructed in 1889 by the McLaughlin brothers for use as a store. It was also once the home of Jennie and Hiram Mann, a Sunday school, and a secondhand store, among other uses. It was torn down in the 1960s.

Otis Cook took this photograph of the Fourth of July parade in 1920. The parade headed west down Washington Street with the Fuel Theatre at far left (later Peoria Fire Station No. 1), the Blue Mill Café building (by 1920 a post office, grocery store, and the office of the *Peoria Enterprise* newspaper), and the Edwards Hotel at far right.

Peoria's commercial district along Washington Street between Grand and Eighty-third Avenues took on an air of permanence with its row of new brick buildings in the early 1920s. The post office is at the far left. In 2010, the Pay'n Takit building is operated as a bicycle shop.

Jenning's Garage, later Wilhelm's Garage, is one of the oldest continuously operated businesses in Peoria. This photograph from the 1920s shows the sparse yet functional nature of a rural auto supply shop, which also sold farm implements. Mr. Jennings is at left, Opal Cook Davis is at center, and Mrs. Jennings is at right.

The intersection of Washington Street and Grand Avenue was a busy place in the late 1950s. Not only was it home to T. F. Thurston's real estate and insurance office, but also Wood's Pharmacy and soda fountain. The Western Auto store had recently moved to the ground floor of the Hood Building a block away. Wood's also doubled as Peoria's Greyhound bus station, serving travelers along U.S. Highway 60.

The businesses along Grand Avenue benefited greatly from the steady stream of travelers along U.S. 60 until the completion of the interstate freeway system in the 1980s. The bay at Wilhelm's Garage was built to accommodate large farming equipment requiring repair.

This photograph shows the continuation of business emanating from Grand Avenue and extending west along Washington Street in the late 1950s.

This is the same view as the previous two photographs but taken when Peoria's commercial district was new in the 1920s. At far left is Jenning's Garage (later Wilhelm's Garage), and the Hood Building is at far right. It appeared in a booster issue of the *Peoria Times*, when the young town was doing its best to attract new residents who might settle and invest in its future.

Downtown Peoria looking southeast down Grand Avenue is nearly unrecognizable in the 1960s, compared to the previous photographs. The busy road (U.S. 60, 70, 89, and State Route 93) is a forest of streetlights, traffic signals, gas stations, and fast food joints. The Arizona Bank (later a Bank of America), Texaco, and Dairy Queen are memories now.

Heading northwest out of Peoria and the Salt River Valley, Grand Avenue crosses the Agua Fria River. The steel railroad bridge over the Agua Fria was originally constructed in 1908. A flood washed out one of the spans, and a new one was installed in its place around 1921, before this photograph was taken.

Around 1925, the Christmas tree was installed in the train depot, the busiest place in town, where everyone could enjoy it. After passenger service ended, the depot was sold and moved to McCormick-Stillman Railroad Park in Scottsdale.

The Wagoner Mansion, close to Grand Avenue, was a Peoria landmark for decades. It served briefly as an inn and was demolished in 1966 for the Smitty's shopping center.

The Wagoner Mansion was originally the Greenhut Ranch. The first portion of the home was built in 1889. Wagoner acquired the property in 1904. In this photograph and the one following, the original Greenhut home can be seen at right with the gable end and round vent. The bricks were made on the banks of the New River about 1 mile west of Peoria.

In a later photograph, it is apparent that two different architectural styles are employed on the Wagoner Mansion. The simplicity of the Greenhut Ranch, the portion of the building at right, was built out of necessity with very little ornamentation. The exuberant style and size of the Wagoner portion of the home at left expressed the family's cattle ranching success.

The well-appointed living room of the Wagoner Mansion served as backdrop to local beauties Connie (left) and Carolyn Wagoner. The sisters were regular beauty pageant contestants. Connie Wagoner was the first Salad Bowl Queen.

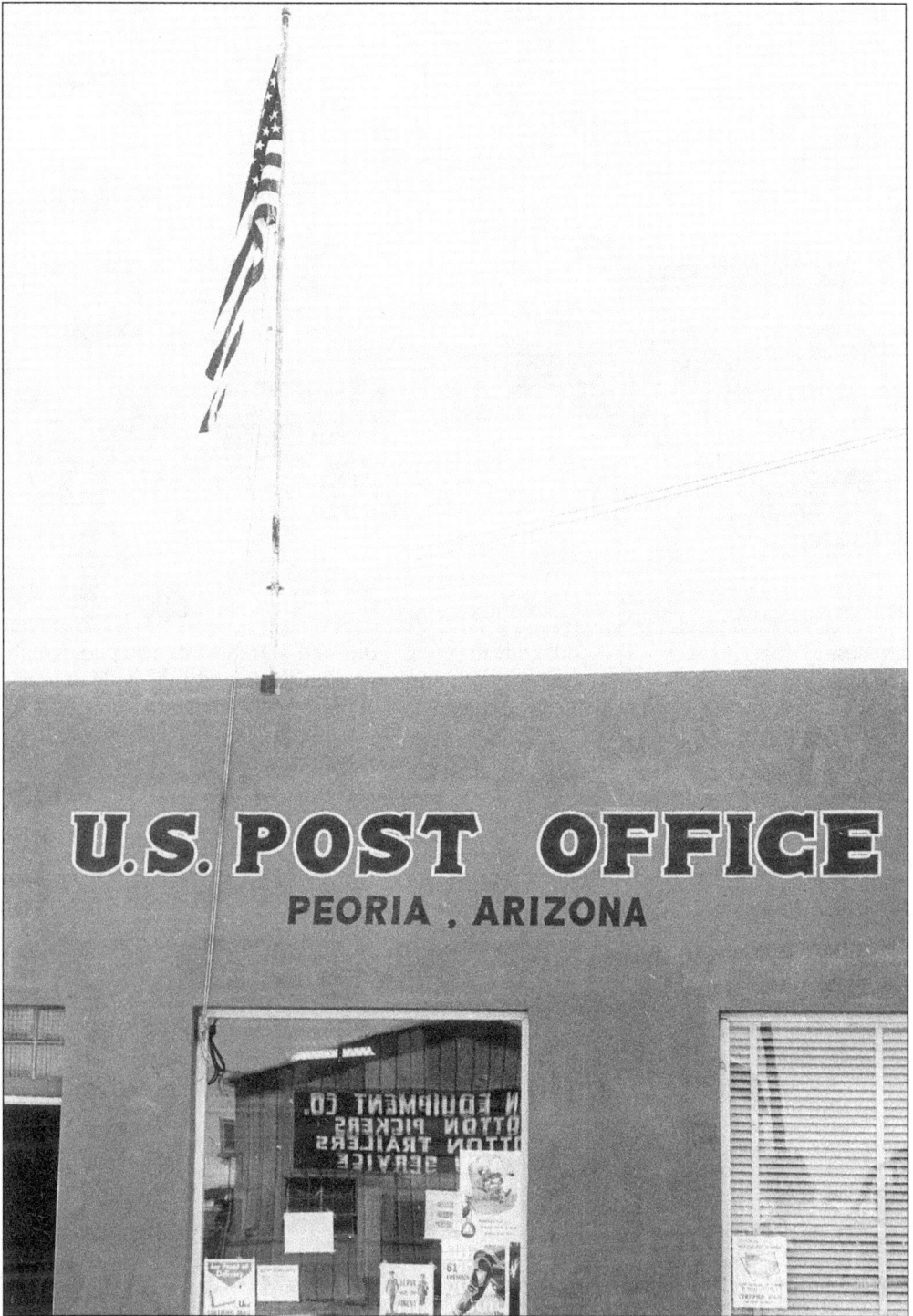

One of the first locations of the post office was on Grand Avenue in the downtown commercial district. In this undated photograph by an unidentified photographer, it is clear that capturing the American flag was the goal of the shot.

Dr. Ross Martin's house was a point of pride in young Peoria and warranted its own photograph. Buildings like this added a feeling of permanence to the town which, around 1920, had just begun building substantially with brick and materials shipped in on the railroad.

John William Forney built this farmhouse at Eighty-ninth Avenue and Monroe Street, west of downtown Peoria. The back of a hog can be seen in the lower portion of the photograph. As of 2010, the house still stands.

The Bissinger farmhouse was another textbook bungalow example. Though the seemingly barren desert lacked a human landscaping touch, homesteaders and other farmers added lawns, trees, and flowers. This touch is never more apparent than in the yard surrounding the Bissinger home.

The Edwards Hotel at Eighty-third Drive and Washington Street, later the Peoria Hotel, remains one of the more imposing buildings downtown, second only to the Hood Building at Eighty-third Avenue and Washington Street.

The Peoria Hotel had converted some of its rooms to apartments by 1960 and also enclosed the second-story porch, used for sleeping in hot weather before the advent of air-conditioning. The Women's Club is the dark building surrounded by palm trees at far left, while the old Flatiron Building stands (painted white) to the right of the Women's Club.

Not much is known about this Peoria photograph from the late 1920s. The block house and cars are typical of the time. The man resting on the porch could be legitimately resting, or it could be a joke on his part. The child in front of the car is unidentified, possibly a relative of the Johnson family.

This is a 1920s view looking south down Grand Avenue. The unusual perspective illustrates the busy nature of Peoria's downtown along a major highway and railroad. The Mobilgas station at left would have been located between Grand Avenue and the railroad tracks, before the road was widened. The buildings in front of the water tower were known collectively as the Triangle or Flatiron Block. To the left of the Triangle and water tower are Wood's Pharmacy and the row of commercial buildings that are still located along Washington Street and Grand Avenue.

Peoria's water tower provided not only storage to meet water needs, but it was also a landmark along the highway. By 1936, its location became a problem, as it stood in the middle of Washington Street between Wood's Pharmacy and the Flatiron Building.

The water tower was removed in 1936. Cables were attached to the structure and can be see faintly at right. The buildings seen behind it are now also gone. The palm trees at the rear of the photograph are located at Osuna Park.

This man, clearly satisfied with his work, is holding the cables that pulled the tower down. The commercial row of buildings on Washington Street can be glimpsed at left as well as the Hood Building at right.

Another angle of the water tower's collapse better shows the Flatiron Building and the Mobilgas station at right.

PEORIA *times*

(602) 979-3722

VOL. 26 - NO. 39   10   SEPTEMBER 29, 1978

Published And Printed By Pueblo Publishers, Inc.

Serving Peoria, El Mirage and Surprise

GONE: BUT NOT FORGOTTEN, at least by most Peorians, are the buildings that stood on the triangular corner of 83rd, Grand Avenue and Washington downtown. The stores are past history, now, however, as the new section of 83rd Avenue will cut across it and connect with Peoria Avenue on the east side of Grand. Staff photo by Ed Mossman.

An article in the *Peoria Times* from 1978 shows the vacant lot where the Flatiron Building and water tower once stood. The view is looking toward the buildings of Washington Street with Grand Avenue at left. Eighty-third Avenue was partially realigned through this area, and it is now the location of Peoria's Pioneer Memorial.

49

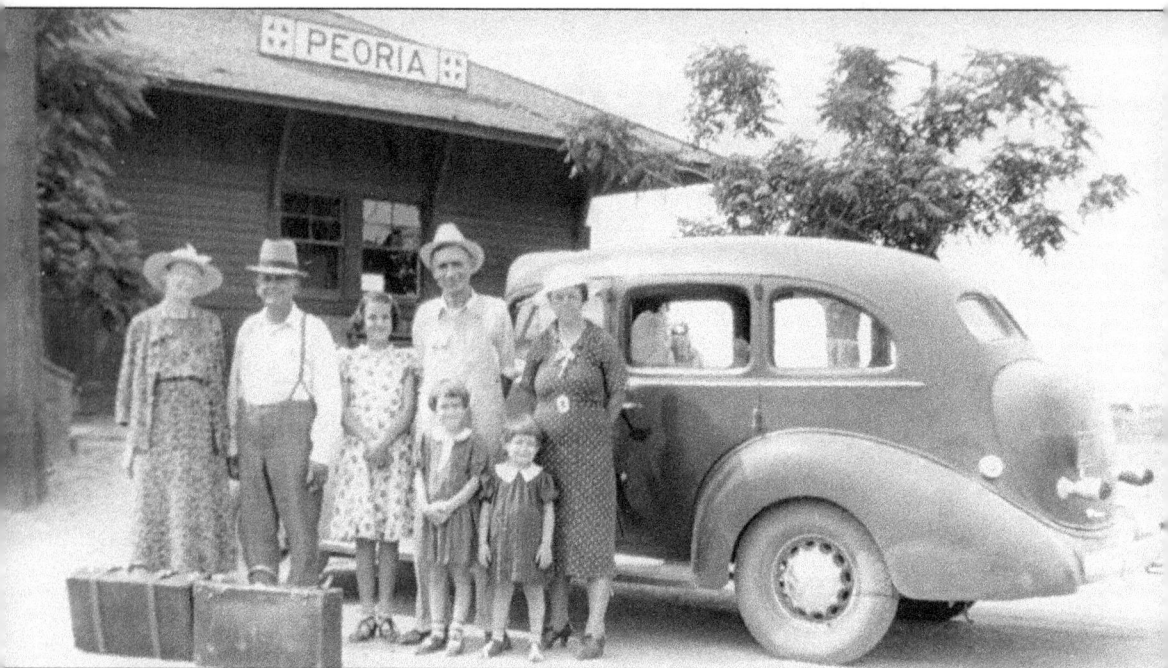

Posing at the Peoria train station in June 1938 are, from left to right, Mr. and Mrs. George Young; 12-year-old Bessie Young; her father, William; mother Katie; and Irene and Lena Grace Young (then four years old).

Three

CULTIVATING THE DESERT

Raymond Johnson plows the fields at the Johnson's Peoria Ranch just before machines became affordable enough for the common farmer to make easy work of cultivation. Animals were integral to farming long into the 20th century.

Joe Puckett Sr. worked at the Peoria Gin, a longtime operation near Grand Avenue and the railroad tracks. Gins were often located close to both truck and railroad routes for easy transportation.

An unidentified man poses with a cotton bale at the Peoria Gin in 1912. A cotton bale can weigh as much as 500 pounds.

The Starr homestead was located at the northwest corner of Thunderbird Road and Eighty-third Avenue. This photograph was taken sometime around 1920. Water towers were necessary to ensure supply and create water pressure.

The Burton Durby home is under construction in 1954. The emphasis in farmhouse architecture was functionality above anything else.

By 1930, the automobile was beginning to usurp the position of the animal as a tool on the farm. The Varney's truck could pull this hay wagon with little trouble at the Cactus Farm near Seventy-first Avenue and Cactus Road.

The Bissinger Ranch was recorded in an aerial photograph in 1955. It was located on the south side of Peoria Avenue and east of Seventy-ninth Avenue.

54

This milking cow once made William H. Young's backyard her home, before livestock was banned from downtown. Young's home was located at 8609 West Jefferson Street.

Ken Johnson poses proudly with the hog he bred and raised. The hog was named grand champion at the Arizona State Fair in 1949.

Carrots are hand-harvested from one of the Conner vegetable fields in the late 1940s. The White Tank Mountains are in the background.

The Conner farm crated its own melons for transport and marked the crates with the Conner label.

This shed at the Conner operation was devoted entirely to sorting cantaloupes. The Conner farm and shed were located north of Grand Avenue along the railroad tracks and east of Eighty-seventh Avenue. Only a concrete slab remains today.

This view of the rear of the packing shed around 1949 offers a glimpse of how the crated melons were transferred to market overland. A truck carried the ice, which was necessary to keep the produce from spoiling before it could get to market.

The Valley Gin was one of Peoria's larger agricultural enterprises around 1960. Grand Avenue is in the bottom of the photograph while Eighty-third Avenue runs along the top adjacent to the line of oleanders.

D. O. Essly, standing at left, directs cotton prior to weighing at the Valley Gin in 1935. Peoria was once home to as many as five gins before the market dipped in 1920.

Two of the control panels at the Valley Gin can be seen here in the 1950s. By the 1950s, cotton processing was a technologically advanced industry, compared to the photograph at the top of the page.

After debris such as dirt and plant material is removed through a cleaning machine, cotton is sent through a large dryer like this one at the Valley Gin around 1955.

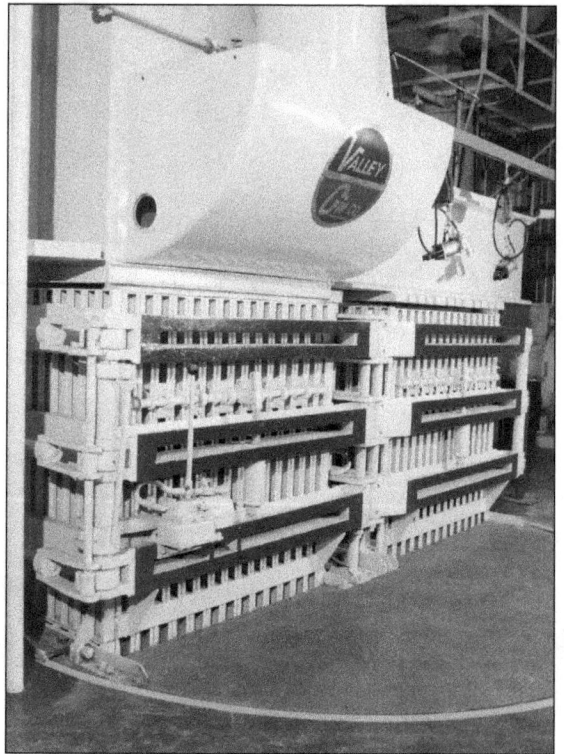

A cotton bale press is seen here at the Valley Gin in the 1950s. By the middle of the 20th century, cotton processing was almost completely mechanized. The word "gin" is short for "engine," after Eli Whitney's invention, the "Little Cotton Engine."

This aerial view is looking east at the Valley Gin with Grand Avenue at the bottom of the photograph and Eighty-third Avenue at the left, prior to its realignment. A portion of downtown is also visible at the bottom of the photograph.

This final view of the Valley Gin shows the extent of the operation. Acres of land are covered in baled cotton both southeast and north of the main complex of buildings. Downtown Peoria is at the upper left of the photograph, including the Peoria Central School property.

Crop dusters, like the one seen in this 1960 photograph, were fairly insubstantial planes. Dusting removes the leaves from the cotton, making it easier to harvest the cotton bolls.

The Mothershed Crop Dusting Company was owned by Caldwell "C. C." Mothershed, a former instructor at Thunderbird Field (now the Thunderbird School of Global Management).

C. C. Mothershed (center) poses two unidentified women and one of his planes. Mothershed operated his crop dusting company for 26 years.

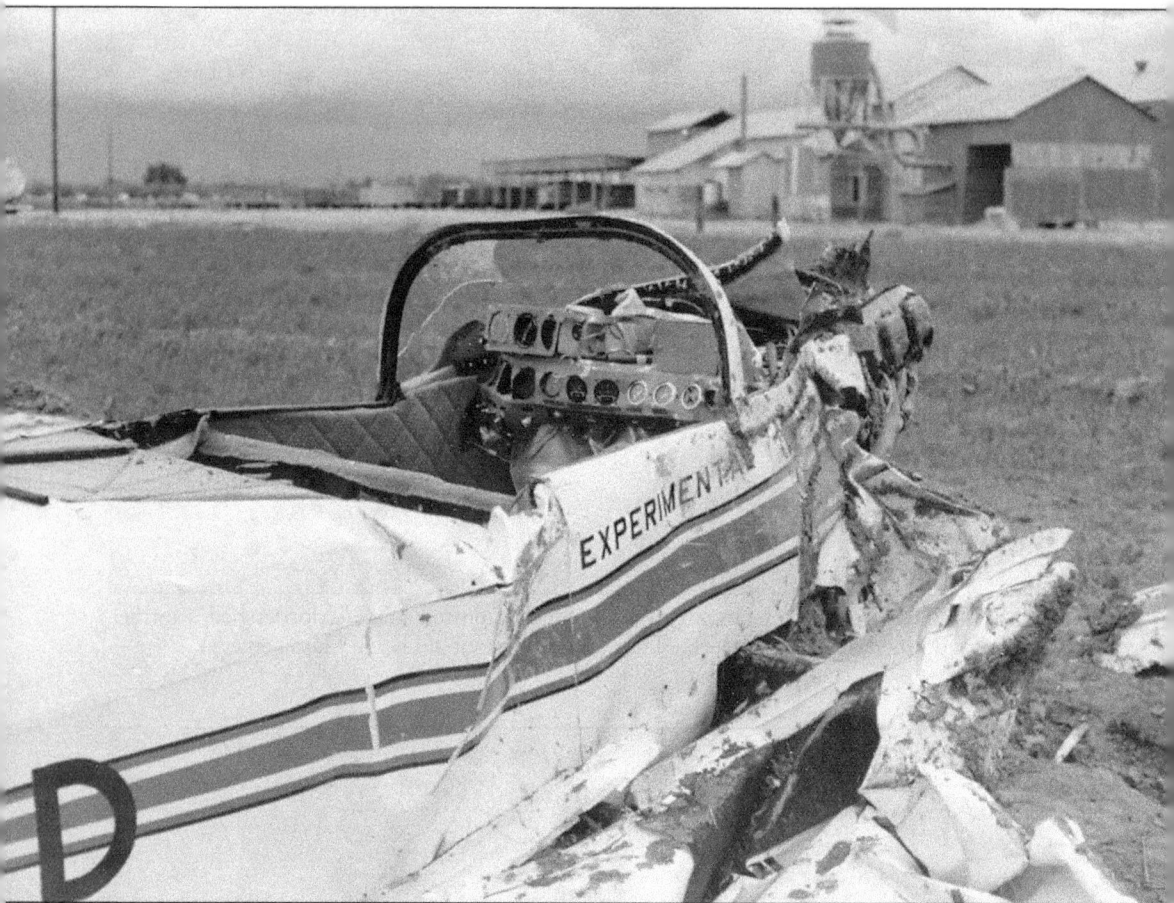

An experimental plane crashed near Patterson's Gin in October 1974. The former Glendale Airport was once located at Olive Avenue and Seventy-ninth Avenue. Its short runway made for dangerous take-offs toward downtown Peoria and necessitated its move further west in the late 1970s.

Before tract neighborhoods supplanted farm fields, fields offered emergency landing opportunities to pilots. According to a National Transportation Safety Board report, the pilot survived the accident.

This unidentified cotton farming and ginning operation relied on windmills to supply well water to irrigate their crops prior to 1920.

Two long rows of baled cotton seemingly go on forever in this photograph taken at an unidentified cotton gin in Peoria.

An unidentified man poses in front of an unidentified Peoria ginning operation sometime in the 1930s. Cotton ginning was a dusty process, often coating nearby vehicles and buildings with dirt and lint.

Trailers full of cotton wait to be baled at the gin. Washington Street's row of commercial buildings can be seen in the background at left and the Peoria Depot is at center.

Another view of the trailers full of cotton faces east near Grand Avenue and the railroad tracks at the Peoria Gin, adjacent to downtown Peoria.

Looking south at the gin, downtown Peoria and Grand Avenue appear at far right. It took an acre of cotton to fill one trailer with 1,500 pounds of cotton for the gin.

A large storm brewed south of the former Glendale Airport sometime in the 1970s. The runway can be glimpsed toward the right center of the photograph where it terminated at Grand Avenue. Salt River Project's Agua Fria Power Plant is at far left.

A hot air balloon advertising Rodeway Inn was grounded after running out of fuel in November 1974. The Agua Fria Power Plant, operated by Salt River Project and constructed in 1957 at Seventy-fifth Avenue and Northern Avenue, is in the background.

This is another view of the Rodeway Inn balloon on its November 1974 flight near Peoria.

Four

A FAIRYLAND OF BUSINESS

In a *Peoria Enterprise* newspaper article on April 30, 1920, Peoria's new downtown (rebuilt after the 1917 fire) was touted as a "Fairyland of Business." Nearly anything a homesteader, farmer, rancher, merchant, banker, or doctor could ask for could be found in Peoria. The Deatsch Brothers Mercantile was one such place of business that offered nearly everything, or could send for it by mail order.

The Edwards Services Station was located in the Flatiron Building between Washington Street and Grand Avenue. The station was at the eastern end of the triangle and could service travelers or people doing business downtown.

Men pose with a race car around 1930 at Wilhelm's Garage on Grand Avenue. Wilhelm's Garage remains in business with multiple locations in the valley.

In July 1917, a fire devastated the downtown commercial district. Store owners had not yet embraced brick as the preferred building material, most likely because of the increased expense of demolishing then rebuilding their perfectly good wooden buildings. After the fire, however, fire-resistant brick became the building material of choice.

From left to right are Charles Kenneth (Vic) Vickery, owner and operator of Wood's Pharmacy, and Gladys Shard Christenson around 1950. Vickery co-owned the pharmacy with his wife, Berma.

The Sun Maid grocery store was directly west of Wood's Pharmacy along Washington Street. It opened in 1934 and closed with the retirement of owner Ed Tang in 1998.

Pat Coor's barbershop was a diminutive operation in 1955, but that did not make it any less popular. The barbershop was located on Eighty-third Drive north of the Peoria jail. Before this, his shop was located in the Flatiron Building.

The Peoria-Phoenix Transfer Company, operated by the Muldner family, hauled the big shipments other carriers could not. Notice the three axles under this truck, pictured here around 1935.

The Muldner name can be seen at the bottom of the truck's windshield of this Peoria-Phoenix Transfer Company truck.

The Peoria-Phoenix Transfer Company is seen here with a large load of baled cotton. Notice the driver standing on the truck's running board.

In 1917, trucking companies, as they are known today, were in their infant stages. Trucks more closely resembled tractor/wagon hybrids. Gus C. Muldner, seen here, was the owner of the first 2-ton truck in Phoenix. Note the coach lights (headlights) mounted on the truck, the crank below the radiator, and the wagonload it is pulling. The truck had to be delivered via the railroad. This photograph is at the Arizona Flour Mills building in downtown Phoenix.

No. 12 of the Peoria-Phoenix Transfer Company fleet got into a bit of trouble hauling a storage tank through the mud around 1930. The Peoria-Phoenix Transfer Company, operated by the Muldner family, had its headquarters at Madison Street and Grand Avenue.

The Gus Muldner and his son Carl founded the Peoria-Phoenix Transfer Company in 1921. At that time, they hauled cotton and cotton seed, as seen in this 1924 photograph.

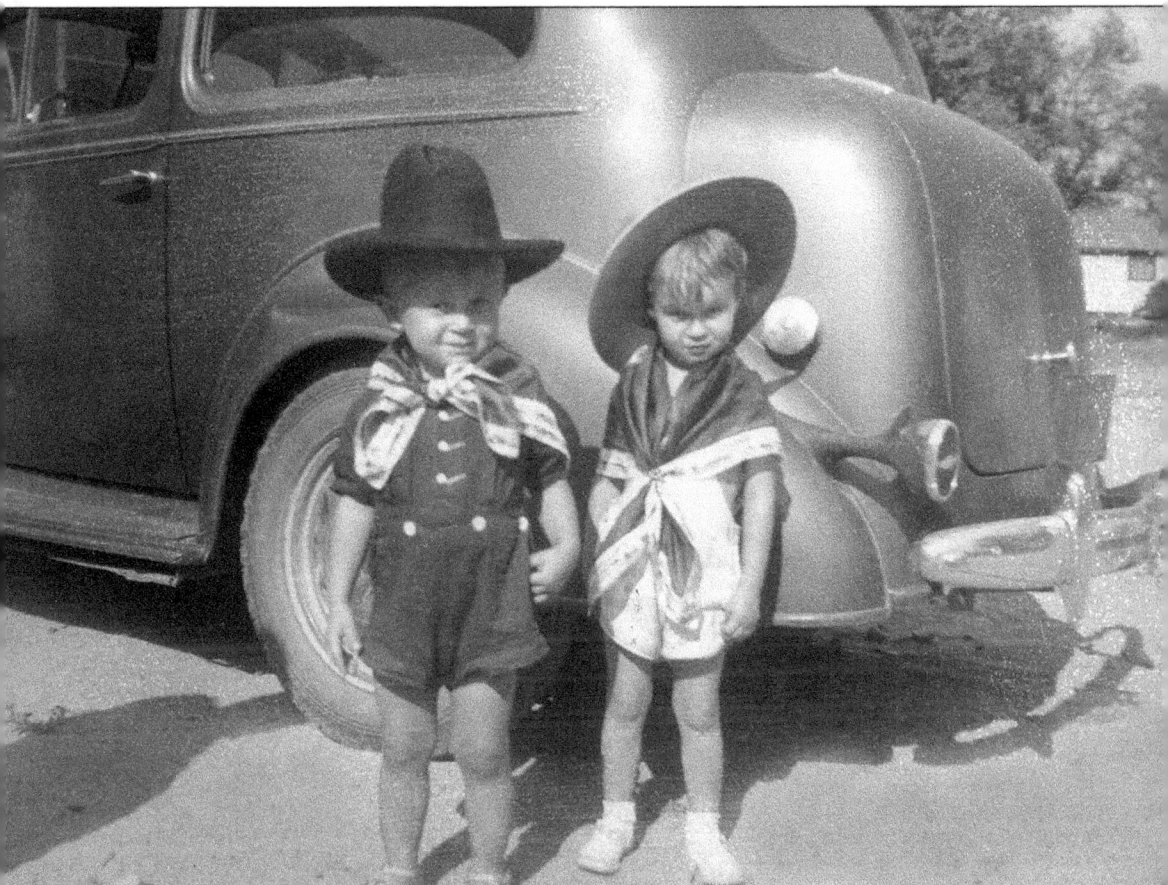

From left to right are Bob Turner and Marjorie Forney, duded out near the family car around 1940. Bob grew up to follow in his father Francis's footsteps by becoming a builder.

The one-screen Peoria Theatre (also known as the Paramount Theatre and the Fuel Theatre) was completed in August 1920. The first film shown was *The Miracle Man* (1919) starring Lon Chaney Sr., with a comedy short by Fatty Arbuckle. The building suffered a fire in the late 1940s. Sybil and O. K. Leonard purchased the building and rehabilitated it. They reopened the theater in 1947.

The Peoria Theatre reopened on February 13, 1947, with a substantial marquee and redesigned ticket booth. The Blue Mill Café, once the oldest building in Peoria, can be seen at right. The Peoria Theatre building later became Fire Station No. 1 in the late 1950s. The man is unidentified.

The two-story Hood Building (built 1920) at Washington Street and Eighty-third Avenue had large storefront windows used by Ben Anderson's Hardware Store to showcase goods for sale. During World War II, the windows were used to display the photographs of local soldiers and to persuade shoppers to buy war bonds.

Saliba's Park and Shop at the southeast corner of Washington Street and Eighty-third Avenue was well stocked and waiting for customers. Owner Jim Saliba is third from right.

Hopalong Cassidy made a promotional stop at Saliba's grand opening in April 1951. Behind Hoppy and his horse Topper, is the Flatiron Building, which was torn down in the 1970s.

As part of Saliba's grand opening, a large display of Folger's coffee was erected at the front of the store. The man standing at left dispensed samples of the beverage.

Another view of Saliba's interior shows customers in line to sample pancakes as part of the grand opening festivities in April 1951. Maple syrup is on the counter at the left.

An unidentified worker at Saliba's Park and Shop stands next to a display of ketchup, chili, and meatballs. Jell-O and Cracker Jacks are at far left. Two cans of Dennison's chili cost 25¢.

An unidentified man poses next to Durkee's "oleomargarine," which sold for 35¢ a box. Cans of Meeter's sauerkraut can be seen at far right. Born in Lebanon, Jim Saliba was a grocer for 50 years. He retired and sold Saliba's Park and Shop in 1979.

Five

CIVIC DUTY AND EVENTS

In the 1930s, the Peoria Post Office was located mid-block between Eighty-third and Grand Avenues on the south side of Washington Street. Teresa Hightower, clerk, and John M. Turner, postmaster, had a brief moment to pose for a photograph. The post office was established on August 4, 188, with James McMillan as postmaster.

During a parade in downtown Peoria in the 1960s, the fire department rolled out its No. 2 truck. The Greyhound stop at Washington Street and Grand Avenue is visible in the background.

At the same unidentified parade, the emergency response van drove south down Eighty-third Avenue next to Saliba's Park and Shop while citizens look on.

A serious fire at one of Peoria's cotton gins around 1970 brought the fire department.

With the smoldering fire under control, the firemen had a moment to assess the situation after the danger had subsided.

As part of Fire Prevention Week in October 1983, the Peoria Fire Department held events at the Kmart on Grand Avenue.

Other first responders from surrounding municipalities participated in Fire Prevention Week in 1983 at the Kmart on Grand Avenue. The Kmart building as of 2010 is occupied by a Goodwill store.

A U.S. Air Force crash truck from Luke Air Force Base participated in Fire Prevention Week in 1983. Vehicles were also on display at the former Valley West Mall at Fifty-ninth and Northern Avenues in Glendale.

A truck from the El Mirage Fire Department appeared during Fire Prevention Week festivities at the Kmart on Grand Avenue in 1983.

The city council members, gathered for an informal photograph around 1975, are, from left to right, (first row) Orville Cook and Don Wagoner; (second row) Charles Kenneth "Vic" Vickery, Conley Kosier, Ed Tang, and Manuel Leva.

This 1954 Ford Mainline two-door automobile was one of Peoria Police Department's police cars in 1957. Peoria was not incorporated as a town until 1954, and therefore did not have an official police presence up to that point.

Peoria's first chief of police was Albert "Ab" Breeden, pictured next to this 1957 Chevrolet. The Peoria jail can be seen in the background to the left of the roof's center spotlight.

Don Curry (left) and Cleave Brannon (right) stopped for an informal snapshot in the Washington (now Osuna) Park in 1957.

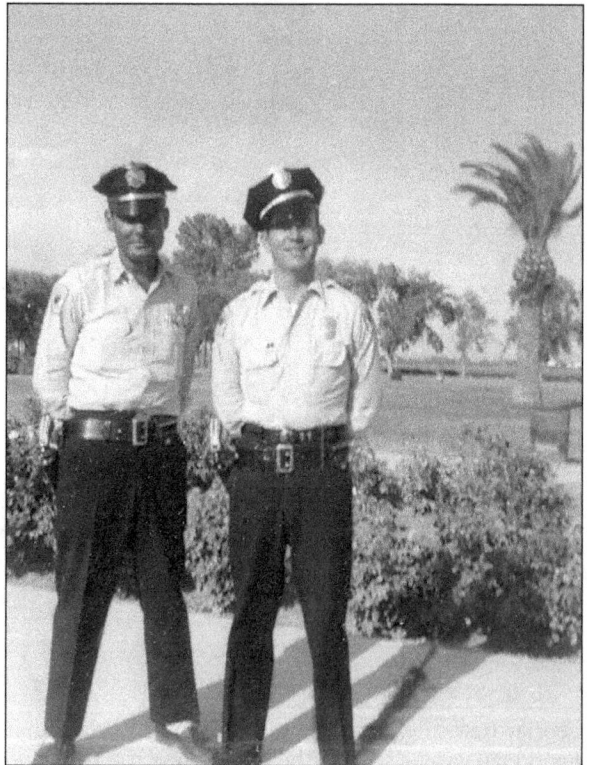

Don Curry (left) and Cleave Brannon (right) stand at attention in Washington (now Osuna) Park in 1957.

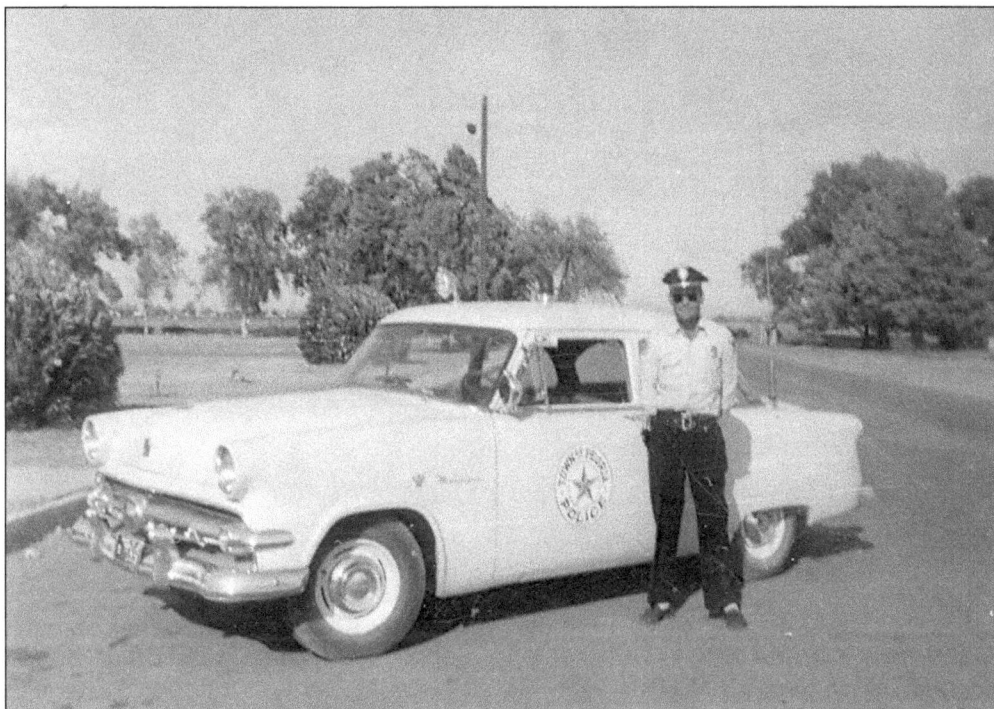

Don Curry, nicknamed Peanuts, was Peoria's first patrolman. Here he stands next to one of the town's first police cars, a 1954 Ford Mainline, in 1957.

An unidentified train derailed on the Atchison, Topeka, and Santa Fe Railway, which occurred outside of Peoria around 1940. A railroad wrecking crane can be seen at far right. A similar steam crane (Southern Pacific No. 7130) is on display at the Arizona Railway Museum in Chandler, Arizona.

Manuel Leyva sits behind the wheel of a 1930 fire truck with retired Peoria fireman Tom Thurston in 1965. Fire chief Gene Mason stands at right next to the department's new 1965 International fire truck, which cost $17,000.

The Peoria Volunteer Fire Department was founded in 1921 and housed in a small shed just south of the Peoria jail. After the closure of the Peoria Theatre in the 1950s, the fire department took over the building on Washington Street and remodeled it as a fire station. This photograph shows Peoria Fire Station No. 1 around 1980. This is nearly the same view as the Fourth of July photograph on page 38.

The Peoria Volunteer Fire Department posed for a group photograph inside Peoria Fire Station No. 1 around 1965. The firemen are, from left to right, (first row) Jim Montoya, David Thomas, Karl Wacker, Ivan Jutson, Gene Mason, and Frank Miranda; (second row) Jim Pennock, Wayne Bradshaw, LeRoy VanCleve, Bob Osborne, Don Curry, Joe Sobarzo, and Jim Kosier.

The last passengers disembarked the Peoria train depot in 1969. It sat vacant another three years before it was sold by the Santa Fe Railway (now Burlington Northern Santa Fe).

The old train depot was hauled to McCormick Stillman Railroad Park in Scottsdale. The loss of the depot from Peoria's landscape is still talked about today.

Six

PLACES OF WORSHIP

Nazarene Church parishioners gathered around 1945 at their place of worship. The building was located at the northwest corner of Eighty-fourth Avenue and Madison Street, and the church was founded in 1918.

The functional nature of the Nazarene Church is apparent in this undated photograph (perhaps around its founding date of 1918). The numerous windows would have been useful for natural sunlight and air circulation, as was the cupola at the top. The photograph was taken looking toward the west from the property of the grammar school on Eighty-fourth Avenue near the current location of the senior center and relocated Women's Club.

The second Church of the Nazarene was constructed 1946–1948 on the property of the original building at Eighty-fourth Avenue and Madison Street. The building is now more recognizable as St. Haralambos Greek Orthodox Church, which owned it for many years. St. Mary Coptic Orthodox Church recently purchased the church building.

The Nazarene Church parsonage was built on Monroe Street in 1952. Churches often provided housing for church officials and owned auxiliary buildings nearby.

The First Southern Baptist Church was located at the northwest corner of Eighty-fourth Avenue and Washington Street. This building was constructed in 1958, with an addition in 1970. It is now known as the Calvary Baptist Church.

The oldest building in downtown Peoria is the First Presbyterian Church at Eighty-third Avenue and Madison Street, which was constructed in 1899. Notice the entrance at the front of the building and the location of the steeple. A later remodel would relocate these two elements. The First Presbyterian Church originally met in the former Horace Mann House/Blue Mill Café building (now demolished).

By 1942, the landscaping had matured at the First Presbyterian Church. An addition to the south was constructed, essentially making the building L-shaped with the steeple moved to the elbow of the L. Close inspection of the building today reveals the former location of the front entry/ original steeple facing Eighty-third Avenue.

In a later photograph, the Italian cypress flanking the front entrance of the First Presbyterian Church almost tops the steeple. The church is listed on Peoria's historic property register.

Church Manse No. 1 of the Peoria Presbyterian Church was built in the fall of 1917 and was home to Sunday school classrooms and the pastor's study.

The Peoria Presbyterian Church purchased a former army barracks building (note the double roof) in June 1947 to expand its Sunday school class space.

Church Manse No. 2 of the Peoria Presbyterian Church is shown in a 1958 photograph.

The Methodist Church and parsonage at Eighty-fourth Avenue and Jefferson Street in the mid-1930s looked rural with an irrigation canal, livestock fencing, and cottonwood trees. The building was moved from the former Nazarene Church property to the south and set upon a basement.

By the 1950s, the Methodist Church had been painted white, the livestock fence removed, and the canal piped. A large cottonwood grew to its east, a vestige of its earlier appearance.

Seven

SCHOOL DAYS

Peoria's first schoolhouse was built in 1891. This is the only known photograph of the schoolhouse, and the original location of the building is unidentified (possibly near the intersection of Eighty-third and Peoria Avenues). It was destroyed by fire in 1905.

The second permanent Peoria Grammar School building was located west of the corner of Madison Street and Eighty-third Avenue.

The Peoria Grammar School burned in 1926 and a newly designed building was constructed near Peoria High School. The large auditorium hosted school events as well as community assemblies.

The Old Paths Bible School was dedicated July 4, 1918, in an area known as Weedville (after its founder Ora Weed). It is located near Seventy-fifth Avenue and Thunderbird Road and is now the home of Southwest Indian Ministries.

Another building in Weedville was constructed with whatever materials were on hand. Screens kept out the insects while shutters kept out the weather. Notice the carriage in the background. Besides Weedville's bible school, the settlement (far away from downtown Peoria) also grew broomcorn from which brooms were made on site.

Ward schools were founded when populations of school-age children grew but lived too far from downtown to attend the central Peoria school. If the population shrank, the school was closed. The Morgan Ward School was located at Ninety-ninth and Glendale Avenues.

The Marinette Ward School served children in the area of what is now Sun City. The tiny settlement of Marinette was northwest of Peoria along Grand Avenue and the railroad.

Xora McLeod, teacher at the Marinette Ward School, found a quick moment to pose for a photograph near the school around 1930. The remote nature of these ward schools is apparent in the landscape at right.

The new Peoria Grammar School, constructed in 1928 near the high school campus on Eighty-third Avenue north of downtown, was razed in 2007.

The smiling, often toothless Central School second grade class of 1967 was led by Bula Davis. Some of the children present are Susan Ramirez (second row, fifth from left), Alma Rosa Reynosa (third row, far left), Lee Lopez (third row, fourth from left), Tim Wacker (third row, seventh from left), George Gonzalez (third row, far right), Frank Ortega (fourth row, far left), Ginny Craig (fourth row, second from left), David Chavez (fourth row, fourth from left), James Allen Cook (fourth row, sixth from left), and teacher Bula Davis (fourth row, far right).

Louise Duncan Weaver, seen here in March 1965, was the nurse at Peoria High School for 27 years. She graduated from the Good Samaritan School of Nursing in 1934.

The Peoria High School had just been finished when this photograph was taken in 1922. The locally prominent architectural firm Lescher and Mahoney designed the building.

The Peoria High class of 1924 attended classes in their brand new high school building.

The high school cafeteria was an insubstantial building around 1934. Vena Cox (seen here) operated the kitchen, which had been located in the building's basement. It stood on the west end of the campus.

Vena Cox (left) and Anna Petersen Holly (right) kept the cafeteria running smoothly. Cox also had three more women helping her serve the students, plus a teacher who kept the accounting books. The people in the cafeteria and the patrons at the counter are unidentified.

The 1928 Peoria High baseball team was filled with recognizable local names. Members of the team were, from left to right, (first row) Hudson and Hunt; (second row) Cook, Deatsch, Ford, Kintz, Patterson, and Hodges; (third row) Hudson, Wacker, Thurman, Smith, Merit, Montieth, and Coor.

The Peoria High football team of 1930, pictured here, included, from left to right, (first row) Curtis Ehrgood, Lewis Jerrel, J. B. Smothers, Dallas Jerrel, Carl Thurman, and Arnold Hannum; (second row) Lawrence Dysart, James Patterson, Conley Kosier, Fred Holmes, Crip Smith, Harry Heflin, Ned Holly, and Charlie Boone. Barto Davis, who doubled as coach and history teacher, stands at far right in the second row. The school's mascot at the time was the horned toad.

Members of the
1930 Peoria High
School orchestra
are pictured here
with their teacher.

Members of the 1945 Peoria High girls' chorus, pictured here with their director, from left to right, were (first row) Joyce Forgia, Irene Franklin, Diana Warford, Dolores Leviton, and Eloise Wilson; (second row) Carmen Lopez, Irene Jacobs, Lorraine Padelford, Eleanore Nolan, Gladys Sharp, and Billie Jo Vaughn; (third row) Florence Periman, Director Lebs, Betty Jean Moore, V. Price, Reta Mae Butler, Roberta Hunt, Audrey Haig, Verle Jacobs, Doretha Lackey, and Julia Brannon; (fourth row) Nadine Vaughn, Carol M. Geselschap, Louise Holmes, Maudie Reynolds, Geraldine Smith, and Frances Soto.

The 1941 Peoria High basketball team was photographed twice. This shot shows them dressed as they would have appeared before taking the court. The coach was Don Pace.

Another photograph of the 1941 basketball team is less formal and shows the team in their uniforms. Members of this team included Ralph Baskett, John Padelford, Gilbert Fierros, Ralph Wacker, Kenneth Carroll, Harmon Puckett, Louis Coor, Leroy Meyers, Howard Cook, and Wayne Davis.

Loren Powers stands fifth from the left with his hand on his hip in this 1925 photograph from the Peoria High School shop class.

The 1945 high school newspaper staff pictured from left to right with their advisor includes Gale Varney, Mrs. Imes (advisor), Diana Warford, Irene Franklin, Horace Blackford and Luther McKisson at the mimeograph, and Nadine Moody at the Underwood typewriter.

Peoria School District No. 11

REPORT OF Grade 2

Wilson Puckett, 1923

STUDIES	1st Mo.	2nd Mo.	3rd Mo.	4th Mo.	5th Mo.	6th Mo.	7th Mo.	8th Mo.	9th Mo.	Class Standing	County Examin'n	Average
Days Absent				2								
Times Tardy												
Days Present	20	20	17	13	18	20	20	20	20			
Neatness	B	B	B	B	B	B	B	B	B			
Deportment	S	S	S	S	S	S	S	S				
Reading	B	B	B	a	a	a	a	a				
Spelling	C	B	a	a	a	a	a	a				
Writing	B	B	B	B	B	a	a	a				
Arithmetic	B	a	a	a	a	a	a	a				
Grammar												
English	C	B	B	B	B	B	B	B	a			
Geography												
History												
Civil Government												
Physiology												
Drawing	C	B	B	B	B	B	B	B	B			
Music	B	B	B	a	a	a	a	a				
Composition												
Nature Study												
Physical Geography												
Phonics	B	B	B	B	B	a	a	a	a			
AVERAGE												
No. in Class												
Rank												

Edna M. Forney — TEACHER

PRINCIPAL

O. B. Marston Supply Co., Phoenix, Ariz.

Wilson Puckett's second-grade report card from 1923 showed overall improvement as the school year progressed with only two days missed. Edna M. Forney was his teacher.

The Peoria High School's 1949 majorettes were, from left to right, Cleo Moore, Lillian Leonard, Cleo Holly, Phoebe Meeker, and Ileen Dominy.

The Peoria High School gym was constructed beginning in 1936 as a Works Progress Administration (WPA) project and finished in 1937. The honeycomb truss system was one of three used in Arizona buildings. The gym was demolished in 2008. The Peoria Arizona Historical Society salvaged the flooring that made up one of the basketball keys as well as a section of home team bleachers to display in the museum.

Eight

PEORIA TODAY

The Peoria Arizona Historical Society was founded in 1990 and is housed in four of the original Peoria Central School buildings. The Mission Revival main building, constructed in 1906, is the only structure in Peoria on the National Register of Historic Places. The historical society is located at 10304 North Eighty-third Avenue and operates a museum, which is open for tours.

Antique farm implements, donated by Peoria's agricultural families, are on display at the grounds of the historical society. The Peoria Presbyterian Church can be seen in the background across Madison Street.

One room of the Peoria Arizona Historical Society appears much as it did when it was used as a grammar school. Visitors are encouraged to sit in the desks and examine Peoria's educational history through displays in the room. A visit here is a favorite of local schoolchildren.

The agriculture building at the historical society features a blacksmith surrounded by the tools of his profession.

The 1939 Peoria jail was built at a cost of $2,014 by the WPA during the Great Depression. The simple, 600-square-foot building has art deco detailing, which is unusual for Peoria.

The Peoria jail building is part of the Peoria Arizona Historical Society's collection. In one of the two cells, a Depression-era prisoner waits for his release. Over time, the building has also served as Peoria's chamber of commerce.

A constable's desk is on exhibit in the historic Peoria jail. Reproduction wanted posters, along with authentic, period-correct items, make a visit to the jail a trip back in time.

One of the newest buildings downtown is the Peoria Center for the Performing Arts, built in 2007. The building's resident performance group is Theater Works. The building, located at 8355 West Peoria Avenue, was designed by Westlake Reid Leskosky and seats 280 people in its main auditorium.

The Peoria Pioneer Memorial, installed in 2007, is located at Eighty-third and Grand Avenues in a mini-park setting. The setting is fitting as it is the gateway to the historic downtown and also highly visible to travelers along Grand Avenue. The 13-foot-high monument is by Emanuel Martinez of Colorado.

The City of Peoria annexed Lake Pleasant in the late 1990s. Maricopa County Parks and Recreation Department administers the Lake Pleasant Regional Park, although the federal government owns the land. The lake is popular among fishermen, boaters, and skiers. Its proximity to the Salt River Valley makes it a popular day-trip destination. The incongruous sight of saguaro cacti near a large body of water is a novelty to out-of-state tourists.

The New Waddell Dam was constructed between 1985 and 1992 and makes Lake Pleasant possible. The original dam, roughly a half-mile north of the new dam and below the water's surface, was built in 1927. A hydroelectric power plant operated by the Central Arizona Project is located south of the dam.

The visitors' center offers information about the natural surroundings of Lake Pleasant along with artifacts from the area's human past. Homesteaders who lived in the area prior to the dam's construction and dam builders left behind artifacts such as evaporated milk cans, toy pistols, and license plates.

The Peoria Sports Complex near Eighty-third Avenue and Bell Road is home to the San Diego Padres and the Seattle Mariners during spring training, also known as the Cactus League.

A view from the lawn toward the field affords a different perspective of the game. Here the San Diego Padres and the Oakland A's warm up before a game on March 7, 2009, which was Little League Day at the complex.

The Peoria Sports Complex is not just for sports. The property hosts city-sponsored events, festivals, craft shows, carnivals, concerts, and car shows. The Peoria Fire Fighter Charities Car Show in April 2009 drew hot rods, muscle cars, low-riders, and stock classics to the charity event.

BIBLIOGRAPHY

"Accident Report for aircraft N9TD, NTSB Identification Number LAX75FU537." National Transportation Safety Board. https://ntsb.gov/ntsb/query.asp

Buckner, Harold B. *Building for Life: A Condensed 40-Year History of Phoenix Christian High School.* Phoenix, AZ: Phoenix Christian High School, 1989.

Burton Cotton Gin and Museum, www.cottonginmuseum.org

Carriker, Robert, and Melanie Sturgeon. *Historic Resource Survey: Peoria, Arizona.* Phoenix, AZ: State Historic Preservation Office, Arizona State Parks, 1997.

"A Fairyland of Business." *Peoria Enterprise.* Peoria, Arizona: April 30, 1920. www.fcd.maricopa.gov/Maps/gismaps/apps/aerialsorder/application/ index.cfm.

Gilbert, Kathleen. *More Than a Century of Peoria People, Progress, and Pride.* Phoenix, AZ: Heritage Publishers, Inc., 2004.

Granger, Byrd H. *Will C. Barnes' Arizona Place Names.* Tucson, AZ: The University of Arizona Press, 1960.

Janus Associates, Inc. *Grand Avenue Corridor Cultural Resource Survey.* Phoenix, AZ: Janus Associates, Inc., 1986.

www.maricopa.gov/Assessor/GIS/Map.html

"New Waddell Dam." Phoenix, AZ: Central Arizona Project.

Official Glendale-Peoria Directory including Rurals, El Mirage, and Marinette. Ontario, CA: Home Directory Service, Inc., 1954.

"Peoria Community Profile." Phoenix, AZ: Arizona Department of Commerce, 2008.

"The Story of Cotton: Nature's Food and Fiber Plant." Memphis, TN: National Cotton Council of America, 1996.

Visit us at
arcadiapublishing.com

www.ingramcontent.com/pod-product-compliance
Lightning Source LLC
Chambersburg PA
CBHW050654150426
42813CB00055B/2181